A ZOMBIE'S GUIDE TO THE HUMAN BODY

TASTY TIDBITS FROM HEAD TO TOE

SCHOLASTIC

WELCOME TO THE HUMAN BODY

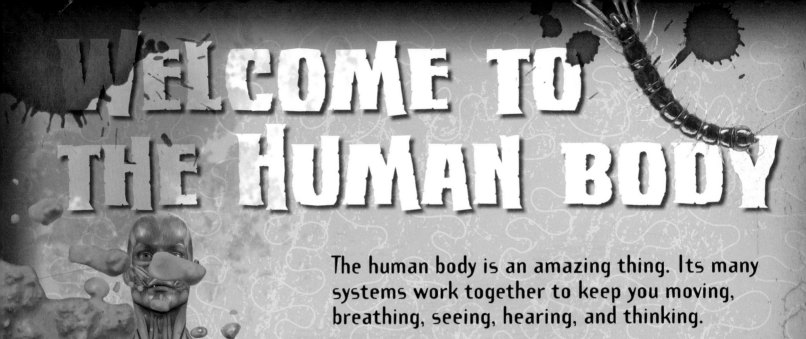

The human body is an amazing thing. Its many systems work together to keep you moving, breathing, seeing, hearing, and thinking.

Muscles, bones, organs, nerves, blood vessels, skin, and more—they all function as parts of a fascinating and complex living machine.

This book will guide you through that entire machine, one system at a time. You'll discover the parts, how they work, and what they do. You just might see yourself in a whole new way!

DEAR FELLOW ZOMBIE,

ME GET HANDS ON BOOK ALL ABOUT HUMANS.

TELLS HOW THEY WORK AND WHAT PARTS THEY GOT.

ADDED ALL KINDS IMPORTANT STUFF YOU NEED TO KNOW.

YOU WELCOME.

PROFESSOR ZOMBIE

TABLE OF CONTENTS

I READ WHOLE THING SO YOU ZOMBIES NOT HAVE TO!

CELLS

Cells are the basic units of life. Every living thing on Earth is made of cells. Some living things, like bacteria, are just a single cell. Others, like humans, are made of trillions of cells.

Cell basics

Almost all cells have the same basic parts. The outside of the cell, holding everything in, is the cell membrane. It's like the cell's skin. Inside, the membrane holds a liquid called cytosol (SITE-uh-sol), parts called organelles (or-guh-NELZ), and the cell nucleus.

Organelles

Organelle means "little organ." These self-contained cell parts do jobs like storing and releasing energy, building protein molecules, or helping the cell reproduce.

INGREDIENTS

ORGANELLES

NUCLEUS   NUCLEAR MEMBRANE

CYTOSOL

CELL MEMBRANE

BLOB   WEIRD STUFF

Cell types

Your body has more than 200 different types of cells. Here are some of them:

GOOD!

Muscle cells

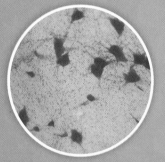

YES

Red blood cells

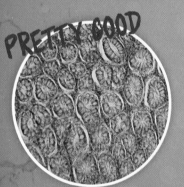

PRETTY GOOD

Intestine cells

Nerve cells
BRAIN FOOD

Nucleus

The nucleus is the cell's command center. It contains DNA, the molecule that holds the code of instructions for all of the cell's jobs and functions. The nucleus has its own membrane separating it from the rest of the cell.

SWEET

White blood cells

Skin cells ✓

Liver cells
TANGY

Life span

ZOMBIES LIVE FOREVER!

Some of your cells, like the neurons in your brain and the muscle cells in your heart, last your entire lifetime. Others, like skin cells, live for only a few weeks, die, and are replaced. Your body also makes new cells for parts like your bones as you grow.

FREE HUGS

118

DNA

This is just a short section of the very long DNA molecule.

Inside the nucleus of nearly every cell in your body, there is a complete set of instructions for building and running a whole human being. The instructions are encoded in a long molecule with a long name: deoxyribonucleic (dee-OX-ee-RY-bo-new-CLAY-ik) acid, or DNA for short.

Recipes in code

DNA is shaped like a twisted ladder, called a double helix (HEE-licks). The rungs of the ladder are made of four different, smaller molecules. The same four molecules repeat over and over in different orders along the ladder. The order of the molecules is a code. It's a set of recipes for making proteins. Proteins are molecules that do work inside the body. They are also the building blocks of cells and tissues.

NO, NOT REAL RECIPES

Decode the code

DNA is in a cell's nucleus, but the proteins are made outside the nucleus, in the cytoplasm. The instructions for the proteins get copied in the nucleus to another type of molecule called ribonucleic acid (RNA). The RNA molecules are "read" by organelles that make proteins.

The DNA in nearly every one of your cells has the same set of information, which is different from every other person's. Scientists recently found that even identical twins have very small differences in their DNA information.

PICTURE MAGNIFIED. LOOK GOOD BUT ARE TOO SMALL TO TASTE.

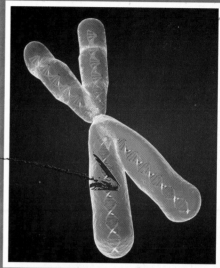

ZOMBIE IDENTICAL TWINS IMPOSSIBLE TO TELL APART

Twisting twisted twists

Stretched out end to end, the DNA molecules in just one of your cells would be more than six feet long. To fit inside the microscopic cell, the molecule is twisted into coils, and the coils are twisted on themselves again and again. The twisted-up globs of DNA are called chromosomes (KRO-muh-sohmz).

SKELETON

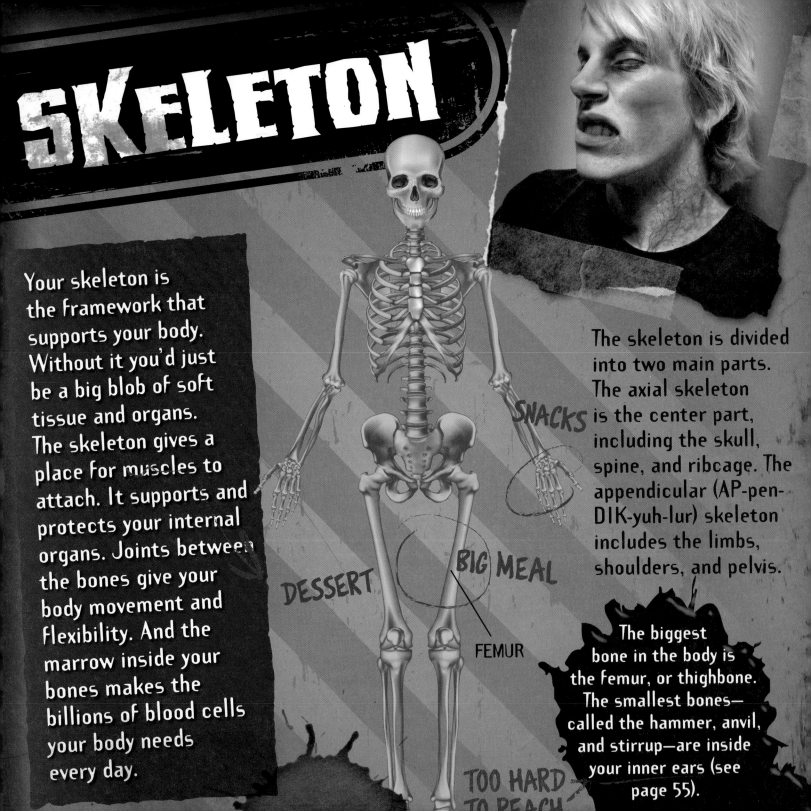

Your skeleton is the framework that supports your body. Without it you'd just be a big blob of soft tissue and organs. The skeleton gives a place for muscles to attach. It supports and protects your internal organs. Joints between the bones give your body movement and flexibility. And the marrow inside your bones makes the billions of blood cells your body needs every day.

The skeleton is divided into two main parts. The axial skeleton is the center part, including the skull, spine, and ribcage. The appendicular (AP-pen-DIK-yuh-lur) skeleton includes the limbs, shoulders, and pelvis.

The biggest bone in the body is the femur, or thighbone. The smallest bones—called the hammer, anvil, and stirrup—are inside your inner ears (see page 55).

SNACKS

DESSERT

BIG MEAL

FEMUR

TOO HARD TO REACH

Long, short, flat, other

Your skeleton has different types of bones:
- Long bones are in your arms, legs, fingers, and toes.
- Short bones are in your wrists and ankles.
- Flat bones include your shoulder blades and most of the bones in your skull.
- Irregular bones like the jawbone and bones of the spine come in different shapes.

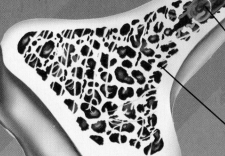

BLOOD VESSELS

MARROW

SPONGY BONE

COMPACT BONE

LONG BONE

Solid?

Bones aren't solid like rocks. Only the thick outside layer, called compact bone, is hard and solid. Inside the layer of compact bone is spongy bone. It's lacy and full of holes. Long bones have a hollow space at the center, filled with jellylike bone marrow.

GOOD ON TOAST

Hold tight

Ligaments are strong, flexible bands that connect bones to other bones. Tendons connect muscles to bones or to other muscles.

REMOVE LIGAMENTS LAST—THEY KEEP EVERYTHING TOGETHER

TENDON

LIGAMENTS

SKULL

To the untrained eye, the skull appears to be a single structure. But it's actually a collection of 29 different bones fused together at seams called sutures. The bones of your skull form a strong, protective covering for your eyes, inner ears, and brain. The part of the skull that surrounds the brain is called the cranium. The cranium is made of eight interlocking cranial bones that enclose the brain and keep it from harm.

SKULLS HARD! COVER UP BRAIN! SKULLS BAD!

EYEHOLE

NOSE HOLE

ZOMBIES!

MOUTH HOLE

Face it

Fourteen facial bones make up the framework for the eyes, nose, cheekbones, and jawbones. The deep eye sockets, called orbits, protect your eyes, and allow your eyeballs to turn in different directions.

Because most of your nose is made of cartilage (KART-uh-lidge) and not bone, only a small hole called the nasal cavity is part of your skull—and not the entire nose.

Jaws

The only part of the skull that can move is the lower jaw, or *mandible*. (The upper jaw, the *maxilla*, is fixed in place.) The muscles in the jaw are some of the strongest muscles in the human body.

On your nerves

The spinal cord—the bundle of nerves that runs along the inside of your spine—connects with the brain through a hole in the base of the skull called the foramen magnum (fuh-RAY-mun MAG-num).

YUM!

FORAMEN MAGNUM

SPINE

GO IN THROUGH HERE OR EYEHOLE

MAXILLA

MANDIBLE

11

SPINE

The spine, or backbone, is made of smaller bones called vertebrae (VUR-tuh-bray). It's the column that supports the bones and muscles of the upper body. It also protects the spinal cord, the main highway of nerves running between the brain and the rest of the body.

SAVORY

S is for spring

Your spine has four curves from neck to tailbone, like one letter S on top of another. The curves let the spine act like a spring, absorbing shocks when you walk, run, or jump.

GOOD ZOMBIE POSTURE

The vertebrae of the spine are divided into five sections.

CERVICAL (SER-vick-ul) or neck vertebrae

EASIER TO EAT

THORACIC (thuh-RASS-ik) or chest vertebrae

LUMBAR (LUM-bar) or lower back vertebrae

HARDER TO EAT

SACRUM (SAK-rum)

COCCYX (KOK-siks) or tailbone

Vertebrae

The vertebrae in the different sections of the spine have slightly different shapes, but each vertebra has a spool-shaped body with a ring of bone at the back. The rings stack together to form a bony tube along the back of the spine. The spinal cord runs through the inside of the tube.

VERTEBRA

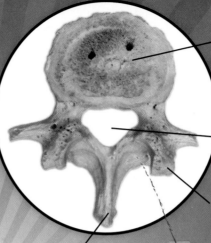

BODY
Lower vertebrae have bigger bodies to support more weight.

VERTEBRAL FORAMEN
Opening for spinal cord.

Muscle attachment point

Muscle attachment point

Flexible chain

Your spine gets its flexibility from joints between the vertebrae. Each joint doesn't move very much, but together the bones act like a long chain that can bend and twist in all directions. In each joint there is a thick pad or disk of rubbery cartilage. The disks act as shock absorbers and keep vertebrae from rubbing against each other.

CARTILAGE

WEAR LIKE RING!

Disappearing bones

You're born with 33 vertebrae, but as you grow, the bones in your sacrum and tailbone begin to fuse together. By the time you're in your thirties, your spine will have only 26 bones.

HANDS

Altogether, the hands contain more than a quarter of all the bones in the body. Hands are strong and useful, yet capable of graceful motion.

Hand bones

In each hand, eight pebble-shaped carpals, or wrist bones, slide smoothly against one another to let the wrist bend and twist. Five long metacarpal bones form the middle part of the hand. Fourteen phalanges (fay-LAN-jeez) make the thumb and fingers.

CARPALS

METACARPAL

PHALANGE

MUSCLE

TENDON

IN HURRY?
SKIP THE HANDS

Muscles and tendons

There are no muscles in the fingers themselves. Instead, muscles in the palm of the hand and forearm move the fingers by pulling on tendons attached to the phalanges.

EXTRA BONES

Sesamoid bones are small sesame-seed-shaped bones inside the tendons of the hand. Different people have different numbers of these tiny bones.

Where you might expect to find SESAMOID BONES.

TENDON

Fingerprints

Tiny ridges on the tips of your fingers help give your hand a nonslip grip. Oil from the fingertips leaves a print on everything you touch, in the same swirling, looping pattern as the ridges. The exact pattern of ridges is different for every person, even identical twins.

ZOMBIES HAVE FINGERPRINTS TOO?

Supersensitive

The skin on each of your fingertips has about 3,000 touch-sensing nerve cells. That's three times the number in similar patches of skin on other parts of your body. It gives your fingers supersensitivity for touching and feeling.

JOINTS

Joints are the places where two bones come together. Your skeleton has more than 200 of them. Most joints are movable. They let your arms, legs, head, and other body parts move, bend, and twist.

YUCK

Smooth move

Inside a joint, the parts that move against each other are lined with thick, rubbery cartilage. The cartilage cushions the bones. The joint is encased in a sac filled with a liquid called synovial (suh-NO-vee-ul) fluid. The fluid lubricates the joint as oil lubricates parts of a motor to keep things moving smoothly. The bones of the joint are held together by strong ligaments.

KNEE

BONE

CARTILAGE

LIGAMENTS

YUM!

Joint types

Your skeleton has different types of joints that move in different ways. You can see how two of them work by bending and moving your arms and legs. Your knees and elbows are hinge joints. They bend and straighten like hinges. Your hips and shoulders are ball-and-socket joints, where the ball-shaped end of one bone fits into a cup-shaped socket in another. This kind of joint lets you move a body part in many directions.

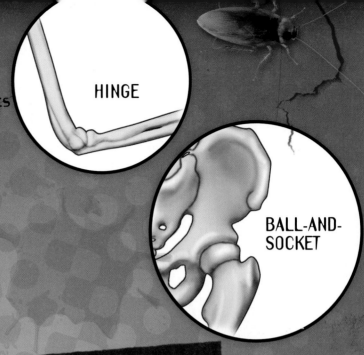

HINGE

BALL-AND-SOCKET

Upgrades

Joints work well and last a long time. But with injuries—or after many years of use—the cartilage between the bones can wear away. The wearing-out is called arthritis (ar-THRITE-is), and it hurts. Some worn-out joints, like hips and knees, can be replaced with artificial ones.

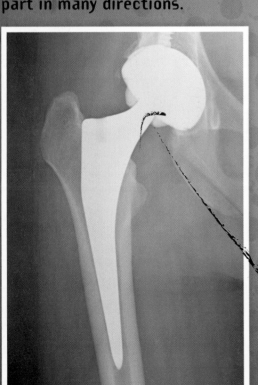

This artificial hip is a ball-and-socket joint,

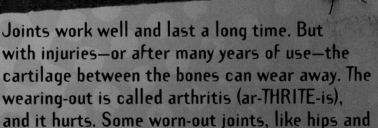

SHINY METAL BONES NOT GOOD TO GNAW ON, BUT MAKE GOOD WEAPONS!

GROWING BONES

Your bones aren't dry and brittle. They're living tissue that grows, changes, and repairs itself. The skeleton of a young person is still growing. It started out much smaller, and by the time you're an adult it will be much bigger than it is now.

CARTILAGE

BONE

OLDER HUMAN NOT SO CHEWY

Cartilage

The growing parts of bones are made of cartilage. Cartilage is the rubbery, flexible material that you can feel in the stiff parts of your nose and ears. A newborn baby's skeleton is more cartilage than bone. The bones get bigger as new cartilage forms and the older cartilage gets replaced by hard bone cells.

Getting longer

Long bones like the ones in your legs keep growing all the way through your teenage years. In the shaft of these bones is an area of cartilage called the growth plate. New cartilage forms at the edge of the plate nearest to the bone end, and the bone gets longer. At the same time, the cartilage at the other end of the plate gets replaced by bone. Eventually all of the cartilage turns to bone, and the bone stops growing.

FEMUR (THIGHBONE)

HEAD

New bone cells replacing cartilage.

New cartilage cells growing.

GROWTH PLATE cartilage

SHAFT

Fuse

When you were a baby, your skeleton had about 300 bones. When you're an adult, you'll have only about 206. As you grow, some of your bones fuse, or join together. Smaller bones fuse to form the skull, pelvis, sacrum, tailbone, and other bones. Your sacrum won't be completely fused until you're about 25 years old.

BONES DISAPPEAR? DONT WAIT TOO LONG BEFORE EATING!

BROKEN BONES

Bones are strong, but they're not invincible. Falls, twists, and other kinds of accidents can fracture (break) them. Luckily for humans, bones can heal themselves. A doctor makes sure that a broken bone heals properly by setting the bone, or lining up the broken edges. A hard cast around the body part with the break keeps the bone parts lined up so the bone can heal.

Right away: A blood clot forms.

In a few days: Collagen fibers form.

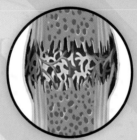
In a few weeks: Spongy bone forms.

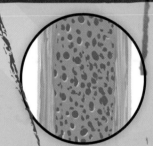
In two or three months: Compact bone forms.

Self-healing

A fracture causes bleeding from the blood vessels in and around the bone. The blood forms a clot, and white blood cells arrive to prevent infection. Then two types of bone-building cells get to work. First, fibroblasts (FYE-bro-blasts) fill in the break with strong fibers of tissue called collagen (KAH-luh-jun). Then osteoblasts (AH-stee-uh-blasts) create new bone tissue. The new tissue starts as spongy bone, then becomes compact bone. Blood vessels grow across the break. Finally, osteoclasts (AH-stee-uh-clasts) clean up the last of the tiny bits of bone.

WARNING: YOU'LL NEVER BREAK THROUGH

Break time

X-RAY IMAGES OF SOME TYPES OF FRACTURES

Different types of fractures have different names, depending on how the bone breaks. In a closed fracture, the broken bone doesn't poke through the skin. If the bone sticks out of the skin, it's an open fracture. Comminuted fractures happen when bones break into several pieces. A greenstick fracture happens when the bone bends and splits but doesn't break all the way.

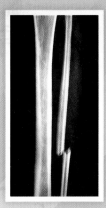 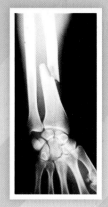 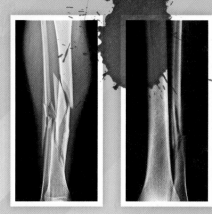

Closed   Open   Comminuted Greenstick

POOR SAD ZOMBIE TRIED TO EAT METAL

HELPFUL TIP: KEEP A SCRAPBOOK OF BROKEN BONES YOU ENCOUNTER

Busted!

If a bone is broken into many pieces or fractured in a complicated way, a surgeon may have to attach the pieces together with metal screws. The screws hold the bone together while it heals.

BOO! METAL HURT!

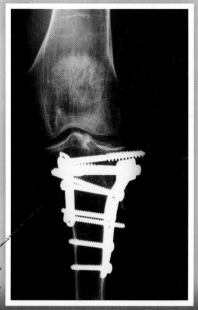

TEETH

There's more to your teeth than you see in the mirror. Only the top part, or *crown*, is visible. The neck of the tooth is the part between the gum line and the jawbone. The longest part of the tooth is the root, anchored deep in the bone.

Look inside

Teeth have four layers. The outer white layer is called enamel. It's the hardest material in your body. Under the enamel is a yellow material called dentin. It's hard, but not as hard as enamel. A thin layer of bony material called cementum covers the dentin in the tooth's root. Soft pulp, full of blood vessels and nerves, fills the inside of the tooth.

CROWN

NECK

ROOT

ENAMEL

DENTIN

PULP

GUM

JAWBONE

CEMENTUM

NOT WORTH EFFORT OF REMOVING

INCISORS

CANINES

The molars at the very back of the mouth are the last to grow in. They're called wisdom teeth. Many people need to have them removed because they crowd the other teeth in the mouth. Some people never grow wisdom teeth.

MOLARS

PREMOLARS

GOOD CLEAN TEETH MAKE ALL THE DIFFERENCE

Tooth types

There are four types of adult teeth. The two pairs of teeth at the front of the mouth are called incisors (in-SIZE-erz). Their chisel shape is built for biting off or cutting pieces of food. Next to the incisors are the pointed canines (KAY-ninez), used for tearing. The next two pairs of teeth are the premolars. Last are the molars. The premolars and molars are built for crushing and grinding as you chew.

TAKE CARE OF INCISORS AND CANINES!

UPPER DIGESTIVE SYSTEM

The digestive system's job is to break down food and absorb the nutrients that supply the body's energy and building materials. It starts with the mouth, esophagus (ih-SOFF-uh-gus), and stomach.

MOUTH

ESOPHAGUS

STOMACH

Down the hatch

Digestion starts in your mouth. When you chew your food, it mixes with saliva. The saliva contains amylase (AM-uh-lace), a chemical that breaks down starch in the food into sugars that can be absorbed by your body. One mouthful at a time, you swallow and send the food down your esophagus into your stomach.

Chyme time

The stomach's layers of muscle squeeze in powerful waves. Inside, the chewed mass of food churns around with gastric juice produced by the stomach lining. The soupy mix is called chyme (KIME). At the lower end of the stomach, the chyme gets squirted a little at a time through a valve called the pyloric sphincter (pie-LORE-ik SFINK-tur) and into the small intestine. It can take up to four hours for a whole meal to pass completely out of the stomach.

When empty, the stomach collapses and has hardly any room inside. But it can stretch to hold a whole meal's worth of chyme.

PYLORIC SPHINCTER

STOMACH

IT'S LIKE MEAL INSIDE MEAL!

Breaking it down

The stomach's gastric juice contains hydrochloric (HI-dro-CLOR-ik) acid and enzymes, chemicals that break down food. The hydrochloric acid in your stomach is so powerful, it could eat a hole through a piece of wood. To keep the stomach from digesting itself, the stomach lining produces a protective layer of mucus.

Going up!

Along with solids and liquids, your stomach holds swallowed air and gases from digestion. You get rid of some of the air and gas by burping. The rest goes out the other end!

THIS GROSS! ME OFFENDED!

GOOD IF YOU LIKE SPICY FOOD

AFTER THE STOMACH

After your stomach has churned and broken down your food, the mushy chyme gets squeezed out the valve at the bottom, the pyloric sphincter, to continue its trip through your intestines.

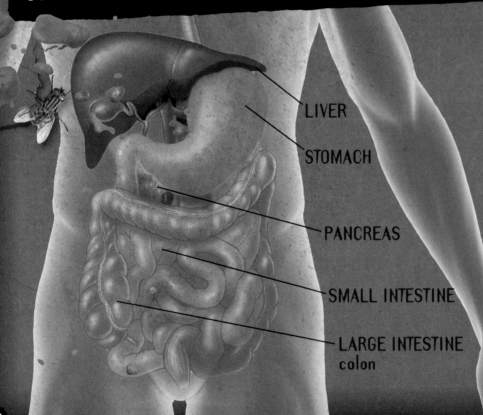

LIVER

STOMACH

PANCREAS

SMALL INTESTINE

LARGE INTESTINE
colon

The small

After partly digested food leaves the stomach and enters the small intestine, enzymes (digestive chemicals) finish breaking down the food into the nutrients your body needs. The inside of the small intestine is lined with millions of tiny fingerlike bumps called villi (VIL-eye). Nutrients pass through the outside layer of the villi into the blood vessels on the inside.

Q: HOW ARE ZOMBIES LIKE ENZYMES?

A: WE BREAK THINGS DOWN TOO!

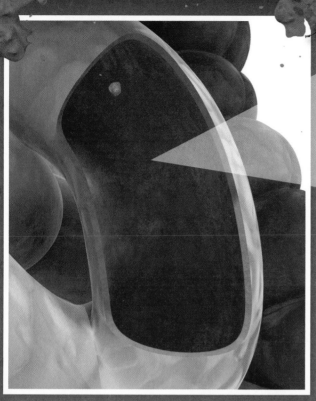

VILLI in the
lining of
the small
intestine

Your small intestine is curved and folded into a mazelike path inside you. If it were stretched out, it would be more than three times longer than your body.

The large

LARGE
ZOMBIE

By the time food reaches your large intestine, or *colon*, most of the nutrients have been absorbed. What's left is mostly water and waste. The large intestine's job is to absorb the water and get rid of the waste. The water passes through the walls of the intestine and into the bloodstream and lymph system. The waste leaves as feces (poop) through the last part of the intestine, called the rectum.

GROSS!!
WHY THIS IN BOOK?

The liver

Your liver is the largest organ inside your body. (The largest organ of all is on the outside—your skin. See page 70.) The liver stores sugar for energy, processes nutrients, and breaks down harmful chemicals.

FOR QUICK ENERGY, TRY LIVER.

27

KIDNEYS

The kidneys are two organs shaped like lima beans in the lower part of your back. They are your body's blood cleaners. The kidneys filter waste out of the blood and get rid of it in the form of urine. They also keep the body's water, salts, and blood acidity in balance.

Filters

Renal means "of the kidney."

Your kidneys filter all the blood in your body about once every five minutes. The heart pumps blood to the kidneys through the renal (REE-nul) arteries. The blood gets filtered by the kidneys and returns through the renal veins. The filtered-out waste and some water from the blood become urine. Tubes called ureters (YER-uh-terz) carry urine to the bladder.

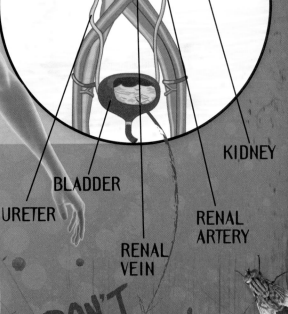

KIDNEY

BLADDER

URETER

RENAL VEIN

RENAL ARTERY

DON'T SPILL!

RENAL CORTEX

RENAL MEDULLA

RENAL ARTERY carries unfiltered blood into the kidney.

RENAL VEIN carries filtered blood away from the kidney.

RENAL PELVIS

URETER

to bladder

KIDNEY

Number one

Urine is only about 5 percent waste products. The rest is water. The main waste product is a chemical called urea (yer-EE-uh), which contains nitrogen. Urine's yellow color comes from a chemical called urochrome (YER-uh-crome), produced when red blood cells break down. Urine should be pale in color. Darker urine means you're not drinking enough water.

Inside the kidney

Inside, the kidney has two main areas. The outer part is the renal cortex. The cortex contains about a million microscopic blood filters called nephrons (NEFF-ronz). The inner, darker area is the renal medulla (muh-DUH-luh). It contains pyramid-shaped bundles of tiny urine-gathering tubes. Urine from the tubes runs into cup-shaped collectors at the points of the pyramids, then into a hollow space called the renal pelvis. From there it enters the ureter.

AND IF NO URINE, THAT MEAN YOU A ZOMBIE

CONGRATULATIONS.

MUSCLES

Muscles move the body. Even when you're sitting still, your muscles are at work holding your body in position, pumping your blood, filling and emptying your lungs, moving food through your digestive system, and performing every other kind of movement that happens inside and outside your body.

Three types

Your body has three types of muscle tissue: skeletal muscle, smooth muscle, and cardiac muscle. Skeletal muscle works your legs, arms, head, and other moving body parts. Smooth muscle works organs like your stomach, intestines, and bladder. Cardiac muscle is found only in the heart.

SKINLESS HUMAN: THE HEALTHY ALTERNATIVE

Skeletal muscles

You can see and feel many of your skeletal muscles from the outside, such as the biceps muscle that bunches up when you bend your arm to "make a muscle." Most skeletal muscles are attached to bones, but some are attached to other muscles. Usually, the muscle is attached to a nonmoving bone at one end and a movable bone at the other. When the muscle pulls, the movable bone moves on its joint. The muscles are connected to the bones by strong, ropy tendons.

Skeletal muscles are striated (STRY-ay-ted) muscles. *Striated* means "striped." The fibers that make up the muscle give it a striped look.

THIS EXERCISE GOOD FOR TENDERIZING

Big variety

Skeletal muscles come in many shapes and sizes. The largest muscle in the body is the gluteus maximus, or buttock muscle. You have two of them. They work to keep your upper body upright when you stand or sit. The smallest muscle, called the stapedius, is inside your inner ear.

SMOOTH MUSCLES

Mindless muscles

Most skeletal muscles are voluntary, meaning you move them on purpose. But smooth muscles are involuntary. They do their work without your awareness, controlled by automatic parts of your brain and nervous system.

Smooth muscles get their name from the smooth look of the tissue, which is different from striped skeletal muscle tissue. Most smooth muscles are invisible. They work inside your body, under your skin, and inside your eyeballs.

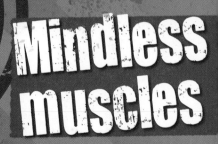

↓ THAT DEPENDS

Moving along

Smooth muscles in your esophagus, stomach, and intestines move food through your digestive system. The muscles in the esophagus and intestines push the food along in squeezing waves called peristalsis (PEAR-uh-STALL-sis).

PERISTALSIS

Muscles behind the food squeeze while the ones ahead relax. The squeeze pushes the food along.

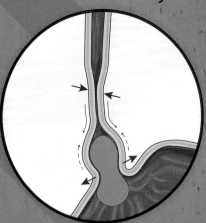

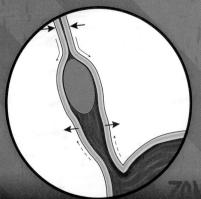

Muscles squeeze and relax to push the food again. Waves of squeezing and relaxing move the food all the way through the intestines, UNLESS ZOMBIE GET THERE FIRS

Smooth seeing

One set of smooth muscles is easy to see in action. They're the muscles in the iris, the colored part of your eye. These muscles make the pupil smaller or bigger to adjust to brighter or dimmer light (see page 52).

EVER NOTICE THAT SCARED HUMANS GOT BIGGER PUPILS?

Other smooth muscles include the ones that focus the lenses inside your eyes, widen or narrow the air passages in your lungs, and widen or narrow your blood vessels.

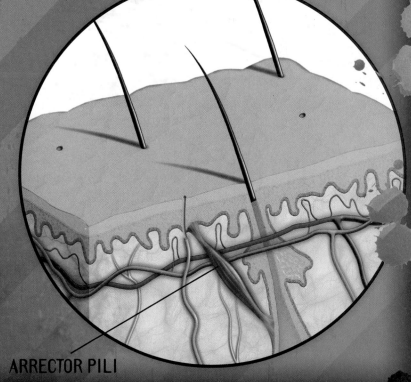

ARRECTOR PILI

Goose bumps

The tiny arrector pili (uh-REK-ter PYE-lye) muscles are smooth muscles attached under the skin at the base of each of your hairs. When you get cold or scared, these muscles contract, making the hairs stand up. That's what gives you goose bumps.

INSIDE A MUSCLE

Muscles are made of millions of long, string-shaped cells called muscle fibers. In skeletal muscles, the fibers are bundled together in bunches. Veins and arteries inside the muscle carry blood to and from the cells. Nerves inside the muscle are connected to the muscle fibers. The nerves carry the signals that cause the muscle to contract (pull) or relax.

BONE

MUSCLE FIBERS (cells)

MUSCLE

TENDON

DINNER

SAUCE

Twitchy

Most skeletal muscles have two types of fibers, called fast-twitch and slow-twitch fibers. Fast-twitch fibers are quick but tire sooner. Slow-twitch fibers are slower but have more stamina and can contract over and over again for a long time.

PROMISED FRIEND
ME PUT HER IN BOOK

Muscle partners

OR BY A ZOMBIE

Muscles can only pull—they can't push. After a muscle contracts, the only way for it to stretch out again is to be pulled by another muscle. So muscles always work in opposite pairs. You can see how this pull-and-relax system works by feeling the biceps and triceps muscles on your upper arm. When you bend your elbow, the biceps pulls and the triceps relaxes. When you straighten your arm, the triceps pulls and the biceps relaxes.

SEE? NOT ALL HUMANS UGLY!

BICEPS

TRICEPS

Biceps pulls, triceps relaxes, arm bends.

Triceps pulls, biceps relaxes, arm straightens.

Pull power

In each muscle fiber, there are parts called myofibrils (MY-oh-FIBE-rilz) stretching from one end of the cell to the other. Each myofibril is made of microscopic threads. Some are thick and some are thin. When the muscle cell gets a signal from its nerve, the thin threads slide over the thick ones, which makes the muscle get thicker and more bunched up.

The names of the muscles are *biceps* and *triceps* (Latin for "two-headed" and "three-headed"). To be correct, don't call them the *bicep* and *tricep*!

BLOOD

SOUP!

Blood is the body's transportation system. It carries oxygen and nutrients *to* all the parts of your body, and it carries *away* waste. It also carries immune system cells that defend against bacteria, viruses, and other harmful invaders.

PLASMA

WHITE BLOOD CELL

RED BLOOD CELLS

PLATELETS

Plasma and beyond

More than half of your blood is a yellow-colored liquid called plasma. Blood cells float in the plasma. Nearly all of them are red blood cells. The others are platelets and white blood cells. Platelets are cell pieces that start blood clots and fix torn or cut blood vessels. White blood cells defend the body as part of the immune system.

CHEERS!

Red cells

Blood's red color comes from red blood cells. There are millions of these tiny saucer-shaped cells in every drop of your blood. Their job is to carry oxygen from your lungs to all the cells in your body. The oxygen molecules stick to a chemical in the red blood cells called hemoglobin (HEE-muh-glo-bin).

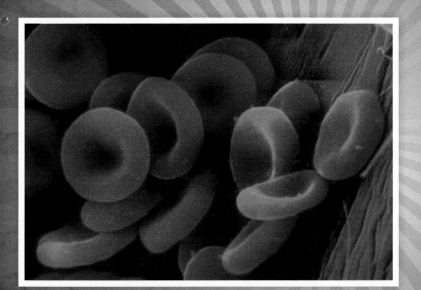

Blood types

Red blood cells have chemicals called antigens (AN-tuh-jinz) on the outside. People can be sorted into groups depending on the type of antigens in their blood. If a blood transfusion is needed, some people can get blood only from certain blood groups. Otherwise, their immune systems will attack the foreign cells.

BLUE BLOOD?

Blood with a lot of oxygen in it turns bright red. Blood with less oxygen is dark red. When seen through skin, the dark-colored blood in veins can look blue.

MY FAVORITE COLOR

BLOOD TYPE:	CAN DONATE BLOOD TO PEOPLE OF TYPE:	CAN RECEIVE BLOOD OF TYPE:
A	A, AB	A, O
B	B, AB	B, O
AB	AB	A, B, AB, O
O	A, B, AB, O	O

ONLY ONE IMPORTANT BLOOD TYPE: SALTY!

HEART

Your heart is the pump that keeps blood moving through your body, carrying nutrients and oxygen to all your cells. It's your hardest-working muscle. It beats more than 100,000 times a day.

HUMAN'S DELICIOUS JUICY CENTER

Pump it up

The heart works like two separate pumps next to each other. The left side pumps oxygen-carrying blood from the lungs to the rest of the body. The right side pumps oxygen-poor blood from the body back to the lungs. There it picks up oxygen and starts the trip over again. Blood from the two sides of the heart does not mix.

Your heart is a little bigger than one of your fists. It sits in the center of your chest, but its shape is lopsided— the left side is a little bigger than the right.

HI

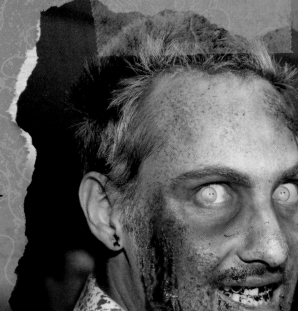

HEART PARTS

RIGHT ATRIUM Receives oxygen-poor blood from the body.

LEFT ATRIUM Receives blood with fresh oxygen from the lungs.

PULMONARY VALVE Blood flows through this valve into the lungs.

LEFT VENTRICLE Squeezes powerfully to send blood to all the parts of the body.

RIGHT VENTRICLE Pumps blood to the lungs to get more oxygen.

DARK MEAT

Lub-dub

Your heart has four one-way valves to keep blood from flowing in the wrong direction. There are two valves between the atria (plural of *atrium*) and ventricles, one on each side. The other two valves are at the exits from the ventricles. The double *lub-dub* of your heartbeat is the sound of the valves slamming shut.

Main squeeze

The heart's muscles are a special type of tissue called cardiac (CAR-dee-ack) muscle, which is not found anywhere else in the body. Unlike other types of muscle, cardiac muscle contracts (squeezes) and relaxes without nerve signals from the brain. Instead, the signals come from special muscle cells in the heart called pacemakers. The pacemakers keep up a never-ending rhythm of contracting and relaxing, all on their own.

FOOD NEVER TOTALLY STILL

BLOOD VESSELS

The blood vessels are the highways that carry blood from your heart to the rest of your body and back again. The three kinds of blood vessels are arteries, capillaries, and veins.

Blood pressure is measured in millimeters of mercury (mmHg). A healthy blood pressure is 120/80, meaning that the systolic pressure is 120 mmHg and the diastolic pressure is 80 mmHg.

Arteries

Arteries carry blood away from the heart. Every time the heart squeezes, a pulse of pressure goes through the arteries. When the heart relaxes, the pressure goes down. The higher, squeezing pressure is called the systolic (SIS-tall-ik) pressure. The lower, relaxed pressure is called the diastolic (DIE-uh-stall-ik) pressure.

THIS WHERE THIS COME FROM?

???

Arteries are shown in red, veins in blue.

JUST GRAB AND PULL!

Veins

Most veins carry oxygen-poor blood on its return trip from the body (which used the oxygen) back to the lungs, to get more oxygen. Only veins from the lungs to the heart carry bright red, oxygen-rich blood. Valves inside the veins in your arms and legs make sure blood doesn't flow in the wrong direction. When you walk or run, muscles in your legs help squeeze the blood upward along the veins.

Capillaries

Capillaries are the smallest blood vessels. They're narrower than a human hair. The capillaries carry blood to cells in all of the body's tissues. Oxygen, nutrients, and other important chemicals pass through the capillary walls into the fluid between the cells.

4 OUT OF 5 ZOMBIES AGREE: OXYGEN-RICH BLOOD TASTIER

Round trip

The arteries branch out into smaller and smaller vessels until they reach the capillaries. Capillaries connect the smallest arteries (called arterioles) to the smallest veins, which then join together into larger and larger vessels flowing toward the heart.

Red blood cells travel in single file along a capillary.

BRAIN

FINALLY!

MAIN COURSE

he brain is the body's control and information-processing center. t sends the commands that control every action, from complicated nes like playing soccer to the simplest ones like breathing. It akes in information from the senses. And it learns, remembers, creates, solves problems, and communicates with the brains of ther people.

Brain divisions

WHEN LUCKY ENOUGH TO HOLD

f you held a brain in your hands, the parts of the brain you could see are the cerebrum (suh-REE-brum), the cerebellum (sare-uh-BELL-um), and the brain stem. The biggest part of the brain is the cerebrum, whose outer part is covered with the folds and grooves most people think of when they think of brains. It takes care of most of the complicated things humans do, including thinking, using language, moving, and processing information from the senses.

CEREBRUM

CEREBELLUM

SEE-THROUGH HUMAN

BRAIN STEM

SPINAL CORD

SKULL

DURA MATER
Latin for "hard mother."

ARACHNOID MATER
Latin for "spidery mother."

PIA MATER
Latin for "tender mother."

BIG HEAD
The brain is the fastest-growing part in a child's body. It reaches its full size by the time the child is 12 years old. A fully grown brain weighs about three pounds and is the size of two adult fists held together.

Protection

Inside the skull, the brain has three more layers of protection: The outer layer is a tough, leathery membrane, or sheet, called the dura mater (DER-uh MAH-ter). Next is a layer called the arachnoid (uh-RACK-noyd) mater. The spaces in this layer are filled with fluid to cushion the brain. Finally, a thin membrane called the pia (PEE-uh or PIE-uh) mater covers the delicate surface of the brain.

LIKE PEELING A BANANA

43

CEREBRUM

The cerebrum is divided into two halves, or hemispheres. The two halves communicate with each other through hundreds of millions of connecting nerve cells. Most of the connections are in the thick bridge between the hemispheres called the corpus callosum (KOR-pus kuh-LO-sum). For most motor (muscle) and sense information, the left half of the brain communicates with the right side of the body, and the right half of the brain communicates with the left side of the body.

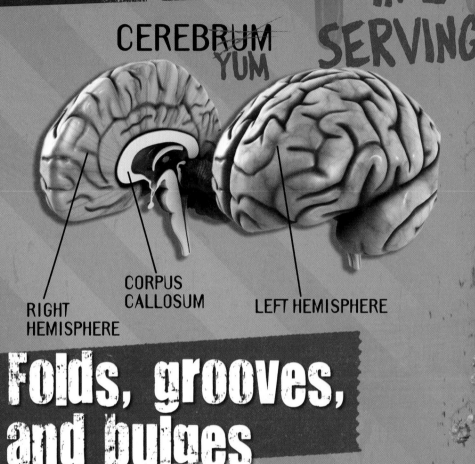

CEREBRUM YUM

RIGHT HEMISPHERE

CORPUS CALLOSUM

LEFT HEMISPHERE

Folds, grooves, and bulges

Most of the brain's powerful information processing happens in the thin outer layer of the cerebrum. This layer, called the cerebral (suh-REE-brul) cortex, is a little more than $\frac{1}{8}$ inch thick. The cortex is folded up, creating the grooves and bulges in the brain's surface. If it were unfolded, the cerebral cortex would be about the size of a pillowcase.

BUT SO GOOD

Lobes

The grooves in the cerebral cortex are called sulci (SULL-kee). Deeper grooves are called fissures. The bulges are called gyri (JY-rye).

Each hemisphere of the cerebrum can be divided into four areas called lobes. Grooves mark the dividing lines between the lobes. Just as the different parts of the brain—cerebrum, cerebellum, and others—perform different tasks, so do the different lobes of the cerebrum.

PARIETAL (puh-RY-uh-tul) LOBE
Processes hot and cold temperatures, pain, and other aspects of the sense of touch.

FRONTAL LOBE
Takes care of thinking, problem solving, planning, emotions, some parts of language, and some parts of movement.

DROOL (SORRY)

TEMPORAL (TEM-per-ul) LOBE
Processes hearing and recognizing sounds, as well as some parts of memory.

OCCIPITAL (ok-SIP-uh-tul) LOBE
Processes information from the sense of vision.

CEREBELLUM

The cerebellum's name comes from Latin for "little brain." It's actually the second-largest part of the brain. The cerebellum's main job is coordinating movement and balance. It channels information between the cerebrum and the nerves that control the muscles, making movements smooth and precise. The cerebellum also controls complicated actions that become automatic with practice, like hitting a baseball or typing on a computer keyboard.

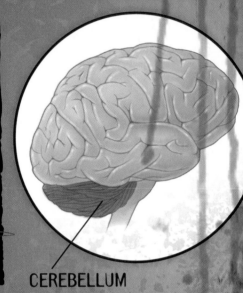

CEREBELLUM

LIMBIC SYSTEM

STUMBLING, SHAMBLING, ATTACKING . . .

Limbic system

The limbic (LIM-bik) system is a group of brain parts that play a role in emotions, memory, and the "fight or flight" instinct that helps us deal with danger. Other limbic system parts include the amygdalae (uh-MIG-duh-lee), which are responsible for recognizing danger and experiencing fear, and the hippocampus (HIP-uh-KAM-pus), which is important for storing memories.

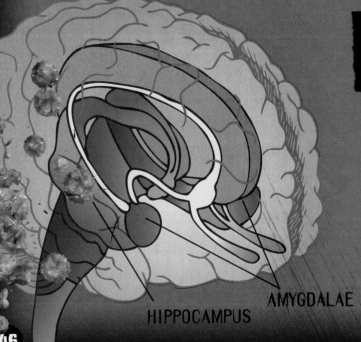

HIPPOCAMPUS

AMYGDALAE

From stem to cord

The brain stem connects the rest of the brain to the spinal cord. It takes care of basic automatic functions that keep you alive, such as breathing and heart rate. It also controls reflexes like coughing and swallowing. The brain stem has three parts: the midbrain, the pons, and the medulla oblongata (meh-DULL-luh ob-long-GOT-uh).

SERVING SUGGESTION: LIGHTLY SALT BRAIN

ZOMBIES

MIDBRAIN

MEDULLA OBLONGATA

PONS

SPINAL CORD

ME ALWAYS SAVE FOR LAST

SPINAL CORD AND NERVES

The nervous system is the body's information and communication system. It is divided into two main parts, the central nervous system and the peripheral (puh-RIF-er-ul) nervous system. The central nervous system consists of the brain and spinal cord. The peripheral nervous system is the network of nerves traveling out from the central nervous system to the rest of the body.

SPINAL CORD

SPINAL NERVES
Main nerves branching from the spine in pairs.

Spinal cord

The spinal cord is the main information highway in and out of the brain. All the information traveling between the brain and the body below the neck moves along this thick bundle of nerves. Your spinal cord runs from the base of the brain, down your backbone, just to the top of the curve of your lower back (the top of the lumbar vertebrae).

TRY NUTCRACKER

NEURON (NERVE CELL)

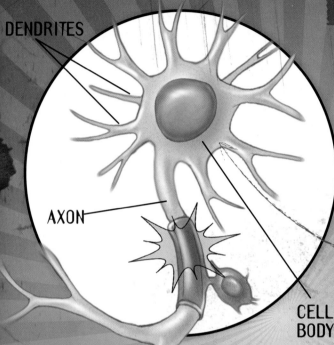

DENDRITES

AXON

CELL BODY

Nerve cells

The nervous system's information-carrying cells are called neurons (NOO-ronz). Information travels through these cells in the form of electrical signals. Signals from other neurons come into the cell through branchlike parts called dendrites. Outgoing signals travel through the long fiber called the axon. Inside your brain are about one hundred billion neurons!

ME SEEN LOTS OF BRAINS—NEVER SEE ONE OF THESE

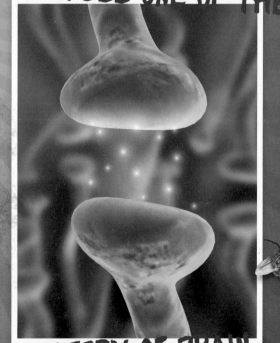

Jumping the gap

Neurons aren't connected to each other. Instead, where two neurons meet there's a narrow gap called a synapse (SIN-aps). When electrical brain signals reach a synapse past the ends of the dendrites, they trigger the release of chemicals called neurotransmitters (NOO-ro-TRANZ-mitt-urz). The neurotransmitters cross the synapse, reach the axon of the next cell, and trigger an electrical signal in that cell.

ME NOT LIKE THIS. TAKES AWAY MYSTERY OF BRAIN.

MOVEMENT

Except for cardiac muscles, which contract on their own, the body's muscles move only when they get signals from the nervous system. The brain controls both voluntary movement and movement that happens automatically.

When I say "Go!"

When your muscles move because you choose to move them, it's called voluntary movement. Most voluntary movement starts with signals from the part of the brain called the motor cortex, at the back of the frontal lobes.

VOLUNTARY MOTION

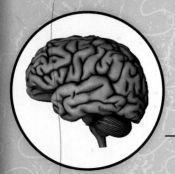

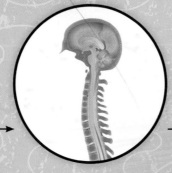

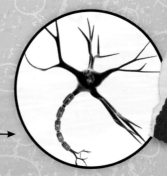

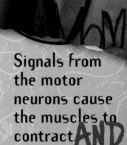

The signal starts in the motor cortex.

Signals travel from the brain down the spinal cord.

The signals travel along motor neurons to the muscles.

Signals from the motor neurons cause the muscles to contract AND MAKE YOU REACH OUT FOR HUG

Autonomic, automatic

GO DOWN NICE AND SMOOTH

Your brain also controls your smooth muscles. These are the muscles that control involuntary movements inside your body. The brain sends the signals for these automatic movements through the network of nerves called the autonomic (ot-oh-NAHM-ik) nervous system. This system works without your awareness.

Tap to kick

Reflexes are quick, automatic muscle reactions. Some reflexes, like the "knee jerk" that happens when the doctor taps below your kneecap with a rubber mallet, don't involve the brain at all. Instead, the nerve signals travel only to the spinal cord and back.

EYES AND VISION

The sense organs are the parts of the nervous system that take in information from the outside world. The information comes in through special nerve cells called sensory receptors. In the eye, the receptors are light detectors.

Eye parts

The eye is built for taking in light and focusing it onto a layer of light-detecting cells called the retina (RET-nuh). Muscles on the outside of the eyeball pull to move it. Muscles on the inside focus the lens and adjust the size of the pupil.

PUPIL
The opening in the iris.

SCLERA
White of the eye.

IRIS
The colored part of the eye—adjusts to change the size of the pupil.

VITREOUS HUMOR
Thick, jellylike liquid that fills the inside of the eyeball.

CORNEA
Clear covering at the front of the eye.

LENS
Changes shape to focus light on the back of the eye.

DON'T BE FOOLED
IT TASTE AWFUL

ANTERIOR CHAMBER
Small space filled with a liquid called aqueous humor.

RETINA
Layer of light-detecting sensory receptors.

OPTIC NERVE
Carries nerve signals to the brain.

EYEBALLS:
NATURE'S CANDY

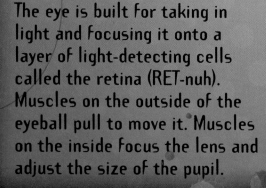

How We see

Light reflects off objects around us. It enters the eye through the cornea, then passes through the pupil to the lens. The lens refracts (bends) the light rays to focus an image on the retina. The light-detecting cells in the retina send information about the image in the form of nerve signals, through the optic nerve to the brain. The brain uses the information to build a picture of the world.

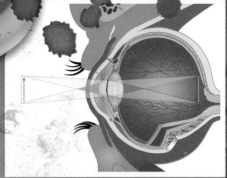

The image projected on the retina is actually upside down. But your brain takes care of making sure you see everything right side up.

Making adjustments

Muscles attached to the lens adjust its shape to focus the image clearly on the retina. Sometimes the lens can't focus clearly, for instance if the eyeball is too long or short, or if the lens is less flexible because of age. Then, extra, human-made lenses are needed on the outside, in the form of glasses or contacts.

NORMAL VISION

The lenses of nearsighted people focus images in front of the retina. Faraway objects can appear blurry. The lenses of farsighted people focus images past the retina. Up close objects can appear blurry. In both cases, glasses or contact lenses can take care of the problem.

NEARSIGHTED VISION

FARSIGHTED VISION

REMOVE GLASS SHELLS BEFORE EATING EYES!

EARS AND HEARING

Inside an ear

The ears are the sound sensors of the nervous system. The receptors are in the inner ear, deep inside the temporal bone of your skull.

The ear is divided into three main areas. The outer ear includes the part you see on the outside, called the pinna, and the canal that leads inward to the eardrum. The middle ear holds three tiny bones that transmit vibrations to the inner ear. The inner ear is filled with fluid. It includes the snail-shaped cochlea (KO-klee-uh) and the semicircular canals.

OUTER EAR

MIDDLE EAR

INNER EAR

WHAT ALL THIS STUFF? NOT SEEN BEFORE

TEMPORAL BONE

SEMICIRCULAR CANALS

EXTERNAL EAR CANAL

COCHLEA

PINNA

Tiny bones

The three bones in the middle ear are the smallest bones in your body. (The smallest is the stapes, or stirrup. Ten of these bones lined up would measure one inch.) The three bones work like a set of levers to amplify and transmit vibrations from the eardrum to the inner ear.

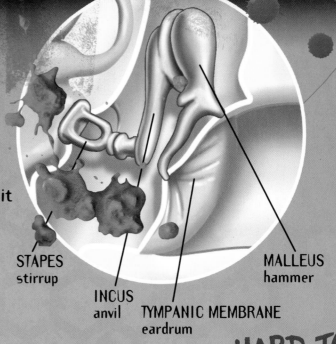

STAPES
stirrup

INCUS
anvil

TYMPANIC MEMBRANE
eardrum

MALLEUS
hammer

How we hear

Your outer ear channels sound waves along the ear canal to the eardrum. The sound waves hit the eardrum and make it vibrate back and forth against the middle ear bones, which transmit the vibrations to a membrane called the oval window. The oval window vibrates against the fluid in the inner ear. The vibrating fluid moves tiny hairs that line the inside of the cochlea. The hairs are connected to receptor cells, which send nerve signals along the auditory nerve to the brain.

HARD TO REACH. LIKE LAST OLIVE IN JAR

The semicircular canals play a role in your sense of balance (see page 61).

(see page 61).

NOT WORRY, HUMANS, YOU'LL HEAR US COMING

SMELL AND TASTE

Smell and taste are chemical senses. The nervous system's smell receptors detect chemical molecules in the air. The taste receptors detect molecules in your mouth.

Smelling

About three inches up inside your nose, a mucus-covered membrane called the olfactory epithelium (ol-FAK-tuh-ree eh-puh-THEE-lee-um) lines the nasal cavity. When you breathe in, smell molecules in the air dissolve in the mucus. Millions of smell receptors in the epithelium detect the molecules. The receptors send nerve signals to the smell-processing parts of the brain, called

REMEMBER TO HIDE SCENT FROM HUMANS!

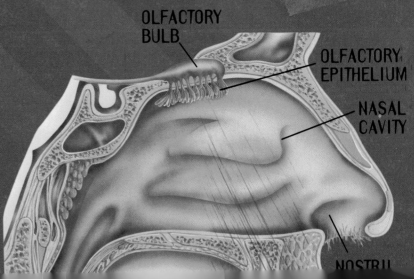

OLFACTORY BULB

OLFACTORY EPITHELIUM

NASAL CAVITY

NOSTRIL

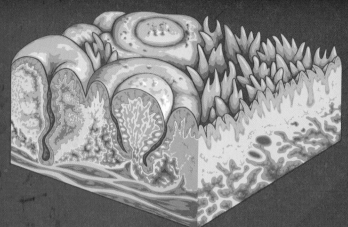

Receptor cells in a taste bud

Tasting

The body's taste receptor cells are clumped together in bunches called taste buds. There are between 50 and 150 receptor cells in each taste bud. Most of the taste buds are on the tongue, but they are also found in other parts of the inside of the mouth and throat.

Different tastes

There are five types of taste receptors that detect just five different flavors. A single taste bud contains a mix of the types. All food flavors are a mix of these five basic tastes: sweet, sour, salty, bitter, and umami (a savory, meaty flavor).

Most taste buds are found on and between the small bumps on the top of the tongue. The bumps are called papillae (puh-PILL-lee). There are many taste buds on each papilla.

MAIN
HUMAN
TASTE

BITTER

SOUR

SALTY

SOUR

SWEET   SALTY

MYTH:
BUSTED!
It's not true that each flavor has its own area on the tongue. All parts of the tongue can detect all flavors.

MYTH: BUSTED!
ALL PARTS OF TONGUE
TASTE THE SAME. HA HA!

TOUCH

ZOMBIE SKIN HAS HEALTHY GLOW

The sense organ for touch is the largest organ in the body: the skin. Receptors beneath the skin's surface detect contact, pressure, temperature, and vibration. They also produce the sensations of tickling, itching, and pain.

Touch types

One kind of receptor in the skin detects light touch. Another detects deep pressure. There are receptors that detect only warm temperature and others that detect only cold. There are receptors for the feeling of pain from a cut, pain from a burn, and pain from freezing cold. There are even separate receptors for feeling fast and slow vibrations.

CROSS SECTION OF SKIN

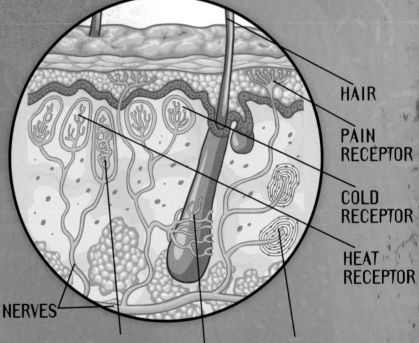

HAIR

PAIN RECEPTOR

COLD RECEPTOR

HEAT RECEPTOR

NERVES

LIGHT TOUCH RECEPTOR

DEEP PRESSURE RECEPTOR

HAIR TOUCH RECEPTOR

SOME ZOMBIES NOT LIKE TEXTURE OF SKIN. YOU GET USED TO IT.

Brain-body map

Information from the sense of touch all over the body travels through nerves to the part of the brain called the somatosensory (SO-mat-uh-SEN-ser-ee) cortex. This area is in the upper part of the cerebrum, just behind the center of the brain. Specific areas of the somatosensory cortex get signals from different parts of the body.

The more touch receptors an area of skin has, the more sensitive it is. Some of the most sensitive areas on your body are your lips, tongue, and fingertips. The least sensitive area is the middle of your back.

BE ON LOOKOUT FOR THESE MONSTER HUMANS!

PERFECT FOR SANDWICHES

SOMATOSENSORY CORTEX

CEREBRUM

This slice of the cerebrum shows body parts drawn next to the regions of the somatosensory cortex that receive signals from them. For example, signals from the foot are received by a section of somatosensory cortex near the top of the brain. The bigger the body part in the drawing, the more cortex is devoted to receiving signals from it.

If people had body parts with sizes corresponding to the amount of somatosensory cortex they take up, we'd look like this strange creature!

59

EXTRA SENSES

If you ask people how many senses humans have, most of them will say there are five: sight, hearing, smell, taste, and touch. Those are the ones we pay attention to, but the nervous system has other senses we use without even knowing it.

Position sense

Deep inside your muscles, tendons, and joints are sensory receptors called proprioceptors (PRO-pree-oh-sep-terz). The receptors are similar to the ones in your skin that sense touch and pressure. They send messages to the brain when the joints bend and when the muscles contract or relax. The brain uses that information to keep track of the position of your limbs and other body parts.

If you close your eyes, then reach up and touch your nose, you're using your sense of proprioception.

Balance sense

Part of your sense of balance comes from your ears. In each inner ear there are three fluid-filled loops called semicircular canals. They are lined with motion-sensing hair cells. When your head turns or tilts, the fluid moves. The hair cells detect the movement and send nerve impulses to the brain.

VESTIBULE

SEMICIRCULAR CANALS

VESTIBULAR NERVE

COCHLEA

TEMPERATURE RECEPTORS let you feel a cold drink traveling down your esophagus.

PAIN RECEPTORS let you know when something is wrong, such as a stomachache when you're sick.

STRETCH RECEPTORS tell you when your bladder is full.

OR WHEN ZOMBIE IS EATING YOUR STOMACH

If you spin around and around, then stop suddenly, the fluid in your semicircular canals keeps moving. That's what makes you dizzy.

HOW TO MAKE HUMANS LOSE BALANCE: SHOVE THEM!

AND A GOOD TARGET

Inside sense

The brain gets information about what's going on inside the body from the visceral (VISS-uh-rul) sensory receptors. These receptors are in your internal organs. They sense things like pressure, temperature, stretching, chemical changes, and pain.

ILLUSIONS

The body's senses are good at telling it what's going on inside and out, but they can be fooled. Optical illusions and other sense-fooling tricks happen because of the way the brain processes information from the sense organs.

Fool your eyes: the changing dot illusion

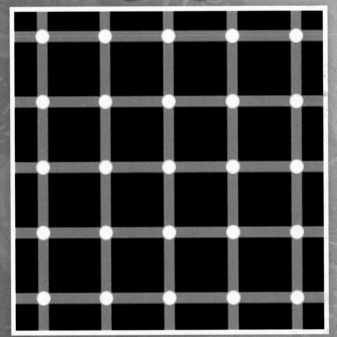

What color are the round dots in this picture? All the dots are really white (look closely at them one at a time to check), but as your eyes move over the image, they appear to flash between black and white. The illusion is fooling the parts of your brain's visual cortex that detect the borders between dark and light spaces.

HOW THEY DO THAT?

Fool your tongue: the apple and onion illusion

With an adult's help, slice an apple and an onion in half (use smaller pieces if you like). Close your eyes and take a bite of the apple while your helper holds the onion right under your nose. The apple will taste like onion. This illusion works because your senses of smell and taste work together. In fact, more of the flavor of your food comes from your nose than from your tongue.

ALSO WORKS WITH PANCREAS AND KIDNEY

Fool your fingers: the crossed-finger illusion

Cross the index and middle fingers on one hand. Now take a pencil and carefully touch the eraser between the fingertips where they cross. If you close your eyes, you'll feel two erasers instead of one. This illusion works because your brain doesn't take into account that your fingers are crossed. You feel the eraser on the sides of the fingers that aren't usually next to each other, so your brain is fooled into feeling two separate objects.

NOT LIKE TRICKS!

RESPIRATION

Keeping your body supplied with oxygen is called respiration. It all starts when you breathe.

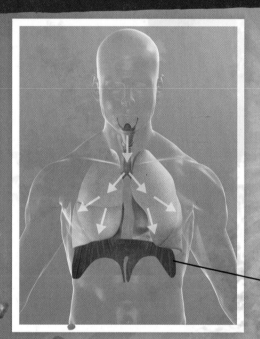

INHALING
Diaphragm contracts, chest cavity expands.

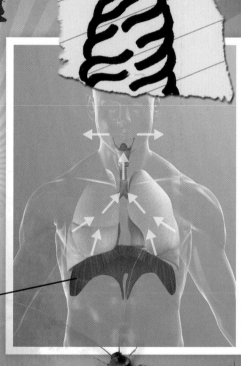

EXHALING
Diaphragm relaxes, chest cavity contracts.

DIAPHRAGM

Breathing muscles

It takes muscles to move air in and out of your lungs. Your main breathing muscle is called the diaphragm (DIE-uh-fram). It's a dome-shaped sheet of muscle at the bottom of your chest cavity. When you breathe in, the diaphragm contracts, flattening downward. Other muscles pull your ribs up and out. Your chest cavity expands, and your lungs fill with air. When the muscles relax, your chest cavity contracts—and the air goes back out.

Autopilot

Your brain controls your breathing. But luckily for you, you don't have to think about it. The part of the brain called the brain stem works automatically to send signals to your diaphragm and other breathing muscles.

ALVEOLI AND CAPILLARIES

SCARED HUMANS MIGHT HICCUP MORE

Oxygen in, CO₂ out

The real work of your lungs happens in the millions of tiny air sacs called alveoli (al-vee-OH-lee). Each one is surrounded by capillaries. When oxygen-poor blood enters the capillaries, oxygen passes from the air in the alveoli into the blood. Waste carbon dioxide passes from the blood into the air in the alveoli. You get rid of it by exhaling.

HIC!

Hiccups are short, sharp contractions of your diaphragm. They happen when the nerve that controls the diaphragm gets disturbed.

ARE YOU CAUSING

ALVEOLUS WALL

CAPILLARY WALL

OXYGEN-POOR BLOOD CELL

CARBON DIOXIDE

OXYGEN

OXYGEN-RICH BLOOD CELL

LUNGS

Your lungs work together with your heart, blood, and blood vessels to send oxygen to all of your body's cells. Together, these organs and your blood and blood vessels are called the cardiovascular (CAR-dee-oh-VASK-yuh-ler) system. The lungs' job is to take in oxygen from the air and get rid of waste carbon dioxide (CO_2).

TRACHEA

BRONCHI

Trees and trunks

Air comes into your lungs through the trachea (TRAY-kee-uh), or windpipe. The trachea branches into two passages called bronchi (BRONK-ee). Each bronchus branches into smaller bronchi, which split into smaller and smaller passages like the branches of an upside-down tree. (Well, this part of your body *is* called the trunk!) The smallest passages connect to groups of alveoli. Each alveolus is smaller than the period at the end of this sentence. Your lungs contain about 300 million of them!

ME NOT GET JOKE

Blood supply

The lungs get oxygen from the air, but blood carries it *through* your body. Oxygen-poor blood comes into the lungs through large arteries from the heart. The arteries branch into smaller and smaller vessels, ending with capillaries around the alveoli. There, the blood gets rid of carbon dioxide and picks up oxygen. The blood travels back through larger and larger veins to the heart, where it gets pumped to the rest of the body.

TIP:
DON'T EAT LUNGS OF HUMANS WHO SMOKE. LIKE CHEWING ASHTRAY! (WORSE THAN IT SOUNDS.)

CILIA IN A LUNG

Cleaning crew

The larger air passages in your lungs are lined with mucus. The mucus traps particles of dirt in the air you breathe. Tiny hairs called cilia (SIL-ee-uh) on the cells lining the passages move the particles back up the passages and out of the lungs.

DON'T SAY NO UNTIL YOU'VE TRIED IT!

LARYNX AND SPEECH

Put your fingers gently on your throat, then swallow. You'll feel a part of your throat move up, and then back down. That part is your larynx (LAIR-inks). It contains the vocal cords you use for making sounds and talking. It's also the place where your trachea (windpipe) and esophagus split. When you swallow, your larynx closes off the trachea so you don't choke on your food.

Voice box

Inside the larynx are two tight bands of tissue called vocal cords, or vocal folds. Muscles in the throat can tighten or relax the folds. Tightening the folds brings them close together. Air passing out through the closed folds makes them vibrate, creating sound waves. You can feel your vocal cords' vibrations simply by humming a note.

High and low

Muscles in your throat change the pitch of your voice by tightening or relaxing the vocal cords. Tighter cords vibrate faster, creating higher pitch. Looser cords create lower pitch. Larger vocal cords also produce lower sounds. Most men's vocal cords are larger than most women's, so most men's voices are lower. Children have the smallest vocal cords, so their voices are higher than those of adults.

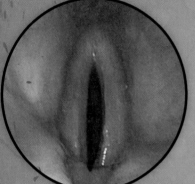
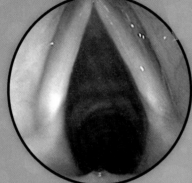

TIGHT VOCAL CORDS   LOOSE VOCAL CORDS

AND THEY CALL ZOMBIES UGLY!

NOT NEED SCOPE TO SEE LARYNX!

Doctors use an instrument called a laryngoscope to see vocal folds.

Yakkety-yak

Talking isn't just making your vocal cords vibrate. Your tongue, lips, teeth, and the insides of your mouth, nose, and throat all work together with your larynx to create the many different sounds of language. By changing the size and shape of the space where the sound resonates, you can make different sounds.

BUT WHO LISTENS TO HUMANS ANYWAY?

SKIN

Your skin is your body's largest organ. It does much more than keep your insides on the inside. The skin is a barrier that keeps germs from entering your body. It keeps you warm when it's cold out and cools you by sweating when it's hot. It gives you information through your sense of touch. It even makes vitamin D for your body when you go out in the sunlight.

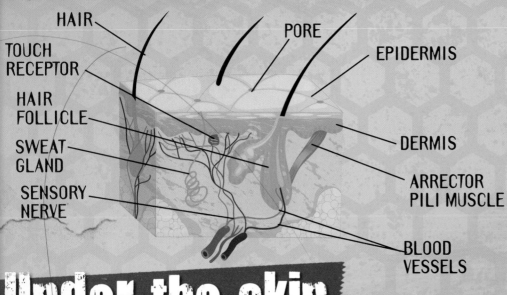

HAIR

TOUCH RECEPTOR

HAIR FOLLICLE

SWEAT GLAND

SENSORY NERVE

PORE

EPIDERMIS

DERMIS

ARRECTOR PILI MUSCLE

BLOOD VESSELS

ZOMBIE SO COLD

Under the skin

The skin has two main layers. The outside layer is called the epidermis (ep-uh-DER-miss). The epidermis grows all the time. As new cells form at the bottom, older cells get pushed toward the surface, flattening as they go. Dead cells on the surface flake off and are replaced by new cells from below.

The inner skin layer is called the dermis (DER-miss). It contains hair follicles, sweat glands, blood vessels, touch receptors, and the tiny arrector pili muscles that make the hairs stand on end.

SKIN MAKE ZOMBIE CELLS??

Hair

ACTUAL ASSORTED HAIRS

Everywhere humans have skin, they have hair, except for a few places like the lips, palms of the hands, and soles of the feet. Each hair grows from a tubelike hair follicle, containing a thick part of the hair called the hair bulb. It's the only part of the hair with living cells.

EPIDERMIS

ROOT HAIR PLEXUS
Sensory nerve endings.

HAIR SHAFT
Dead cells.

DERMIS

HAIR
FOLLICLE

HAIR BULB
Living, multiplying cells.

You lose about 40,000 skin cells every minute. That comes to about nine pounds of dead skin every year!

DISGUSTING AND DELICIOUS!

NAILS
Like your hair, your fingernails and toenails grow from the skin but are not made of living cells.

IMMUNE SYSTEM

WANTED: BODY INVADERS

THEY SAY "BODY INVADER" LIKE IT A BAD THING

The world is full of microscopic invaders that can cause harm if they get inside the body. The skin, digestive system lining, and mucous membranes like the inside of the mouth and nose do a good job of keeping the invaders out. But when microbes and parasites do get in, the immune system goes into action to get rid of them.

WANTED

WANTED

WANTED

WANTED

Killer cells

White blood cells attack cancer cell.

White blood cells are the attack dogs of the immune system. They find and destroy invaders. Different types of white blood cells work in different ways. Some produce microbe-killing chemicals. Some produce molecules that attach to bacteria or viruses like flags, marking them for other white blood cells to destroy. Some, called phagocytes (Latin for "cell eaters"), swallow the invaders whole, break them apart, and spit out the harmless remains.

WHITE BLOOD CELLS SOUND LIKE GOOD ZOMBIES

Immunity

Once the immune system has defeated a microbe, it can recognize that invader the next time it enters the body and destroy it right away. For example, if you have had the chicken pox, your immune system will recognize and destroy the chicken pox virus immediately if it ever enters your body again. You're immune.

Allergies

Sometimes the immune system responds too strongly or attacks a harmless "invader." The response is called an allergic reaction. It may be caused by pollen, pet dander, certain foods or medicines, insect venom, or other foreign substances.

ZOMBIE CAT??!

ENDOCRINE SYSTEM

The body has two different systems for sending messages: the nervous system and the endocrine (END-uh-krun) system. The endocrine system communicates with chemicals.

Chemical messages

The organs in the endocrine system make chemicals called hormones. Hormones are like messages to the body's cells and organs. They travel in the bloodstream. Hormones cause certain cells to start or stop working, tell organs what jobs to do, and control the way your body grows and even the way your brain behaves.

ORGANS AND GLANDS OF THE ENDOCRINE SYSTEM

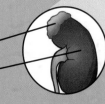

HYPOTHALAMUS

PINEAL GLAND

PITUITARY GLAND

THYROID GLAND

THYMUS

PERFECT FOR PICKY EATERS

STOMACH

PANCREAS

ADRENAL GLAND

KIDNEY

Hormone examples

One hormone, called epinephrine (EP-uh-NEF-rin) or adrenaline (uh-DREN-uh-lun), squirts into your bloodstream when you get scared or excited. It speeds up your heart, widens your blood vessels, and causes other changes that give your muscles extra energy. Another hormone, called insulin, tells your liver to lower the amount of sugar in your blood.

SQUIRT!!

Specific hormones work with specific cells. The molecules attach to places called receptors (re-SEPT-erz) on the surface of the cell, like one piece of a jigsaw puzzle fitting into another.

Glands

The endocrine glands are the organs that produce hormones. For example, the thyroid gland in your neck makes hormones that control the way your body stores and uses energy. The pineal gland in the middle of your brain makes melatonin (MEL-uh-TO-nun), the hormone that controls the sleep cycle.

TASTY FILLING

LYMPHATIC SYSTEM

Alongside the circulatory system, the body contains another network of vessels called the lymphatic (lim-FAT-ik) system. The lymphatic system is part of the body's immune system, fighting against bacteria, viruses, and other invaders.

Lymph

Lymph (LIMF) is a clear fluid that fills the space between the body's cells. It is similar to blood plasma. Lymph contains many bacteria- and virus-fighting white blood cells called lymphocytes (LIMF-uh-sites).

ME LOVE LYMPH FOR VARIETY

LYMPHATIC SYSTEM

CERVICAL NODES

AXILLARY NODES

SPLEEN

LUMBAR NODES

INGUINAL NODES

LYMPH VESSELS

POPLITEAL NODES

Lymph nodes

JELLYBEAN

Lymph is stored and filtered by the small bean-shaped lymph nodes located throughout the body. Lymphocytes concentrate and multiply there. If the system detects bacteria or viruses in the body, the lymph nodes can become swollen and tender as they go to work.

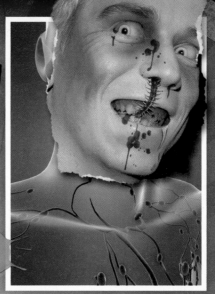

Spleen

The spleen is the largest organ in the lymphatic system. It is a bit smaller than your fist and sits under the lower ribs on your left side. White blood cells multiply in the spleen, which stores them and detects and defends against infection. This organ also destroys old and broken red blood cells.

Groups of lymph nodes are in the neck; just below the back of the jawbone; in the armpits, the trunk, and the groin; and behind the knees.

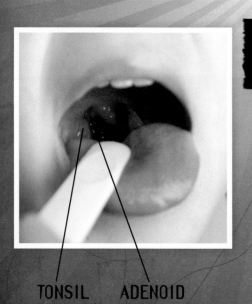

TONSIL   ADENOID

Tonsils and adenoids

The tonsils and adenoids are lymph organs in your mouth, around your throat and the back of your tongue. They trap bacteria and viruses in the air, food, and water that enter your body through your mouth.

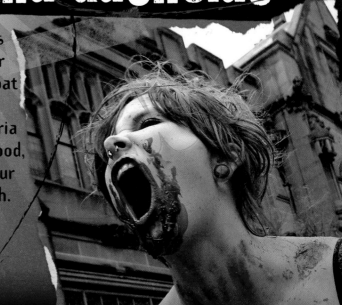

TRY THEM COLD!

SEEING INSIDE

Medical imaging is the science of seeing inside the body from the outside. Different imaging machines let doctors see your insides in different ways.

X-rays

An X-ray machine puts out X-rays, invisible waves of energy that can travel through some solid objects. The rays pass through the body part being imaged, then hit an electronic detector or a sheet of film on the other side. Very solid parts, like bones and teeth, absorb X-rays, so the rays don't reach the detector. The more solid parts show up in the image as white areas. X-rays pass through less solid parts of the body, like skin, and darken the electronic detector or film.

X-ray images show the denser (more solid) parts of the body.

LESS EATABLE

X-rays are like shadow pictures, except the shadows are light instead of dark.

X-RAY AND MRI NOT NECESSARY TO SEE INSIDE BODY . . . JUST OPEN UP!

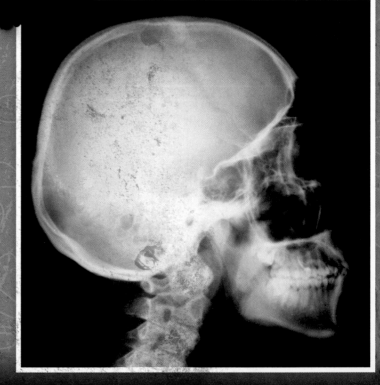

MRI

MRI stands for magnetic resonance imaging. Most MRI machines are shaped like giant donuts. In the machine, magnets and harmless radio waves cause some of the atoms in a person's body to put out energy. The energy takes the form of radio waves. Sensors in the machine detect the waves, and a computer uses that information to build a picture of the inside of the body.

LIKE COOKING SHOW FOR ZOMBIES

Unlike X-ray pictures, MRI images can show details of soft body parts like the brain.

EATABLES

Ultrasound

Ultrasound imaging uses sound waves to make images. The waves come from a wand called a transducer (tranz-DOO-ser), connected to a computer. Waves from the transducer travel through the body, where some of them echo (bounce) off parts inside. A microphone in the transducer detects the echoes, and a computer builds the ultrasound image of the internal structures that caused the waves to echo.

A technician uses an ultrasound transducer to examine a patient's thyroid gland.

LUNCH

NUTRITION

Except for the oxygen that you breathe, all the substances your body uses for energy and the building blocks of life come from the food you eat and the liquids you drink.

FIBER

Fiber is the name for carbohydrate that the body can't digest. Your digestive system needs a diet high in fiber to stay healthy.

Grains, bread, and vegetables are high in energy-supplying carbohydrates.

Seeds, beans, milk, and meat are high in protein.

Nutrients

LIKE BELTS AND SHOELACES

Nearly all the nutrients in the food you eat fit into one of three categories: carbohydrates (starch and sugar), protein, or fat. Carbohydrates and fats are your body's main source of energy. Protein can supply energy, too, but it's mostly broken down and used as building blocks for the body's cells.

Oil, butter, and cheese are high in fat. Fat supplies energy, but it's harder for the body to break down.

Calories

Calories are a measure of energy. When people talk about the number of calories in food, they really mean the amount of energy your body could get if it used all the fuel in that food. Fuel that isn't used gets stored by the body, in the form of a chemical called glycogen and as fat.

ON A DIET?
TRY PEOPLE ON A DIET!

Vitamins and minerals

Vitamins are chemicals that help the body do its work, but they don't supply energy or building blocks. Minerals like calcium and iron are important for the body's cells. Your body gets both vitamins and minerals from food.

There's another important nutrient your body needs lots of: water.

NO SKIP MEALS LIKE THIS HUNGRY ZOMBIE!

EXERCISE

Your body needs exercise to stay healthy. Exercise keeps your muscles strong and toned, maintains a healthy heart and healthy lungs, strengthens bones, controls your weight, and even helps you think better.

U and O_2

Your muscles have two ways of getting energy. For steady exercise like walking, running, swimming, and dancing, the energy comes from a chemical reaction that uses oxygen (O_2). It's called an aerobic (eh-RO-bik) reaction. Exercise that happens in short bursts, like weight lifting, doesn't use oxygen. It's anaerobic (AN-uh-RO-bik). Aerobic exercise increases your body's ability to take in oxygen and work hard longer without getting tired. Anaerobic exercise builds bigger, stronger muscles.

Walking, running, and dancing are aerobic exercises. Weight training is an anaerobic exercise.

WHAT ABOUT BUSTING DOWN DOORS?

Exercise doesn't change the number of muscles you have, but it does make them bigger and stronger. Muscles that aren't used get smaller, or atrophy (AT-truh-fee).

IF YOU FALL DOWN, GET RIGHT BACK UP!

Warm up

Exercise is good for your muscles, but pushing them too hard can hurt them. Using muscles that haven't been used for a while or giving muscles much harder work than they're used to can strain or even tear them. Warming up can help you avoid injury.

Mental exercise

In the same way that physical exercise builds muscles, exercising your brain builds new connections among the nerve cells. Giving your brain a workout with puzzles, problems, or new challenges

Stretching also helps prevent muscle

DOCTORS

Doctors are the experts who solve problems and keep our bodies running smoothly. In order to become doctors, they spend many years learning everything (really, everything!) there is to know about the human body.

A pediatrician (PEE-dee-uh-TRISH-un) is a family doctor who works just with babies, children, and teenagers.

Family doctors

Family doctors give your body its regular checkups and give people the information they need to stay healthy. They're also the doctors you see when you feel sick or notice anything unusual.

Detective work

When your body has a problem, it's usually not possible to tell what it is just by looking. Instead, your doctor has to work like a detective, searching for clues. Some of the clues are measurements, like temperature, blood pressure, and heart rate. Others come from examining parts of your body by observing, listening, and feeling, or by checking the levels of various substances in your blood. Still other clues come from asking you questions.

Specialists

Specialists are doctors who are experts on a particular system or part of the body. Here are just a few of many specialist types: Cardiologists (KAR-dee-AH-luh-jists) are heart experts. Neurologists (nu-RA-luh-jists) are nervous system experts. Orthopedists (OR-thuh-PEE-dists) are bone and skeleton experts. HUMANOLOGISTS LIKE TO EAT HUMANS.

Surgeons

Surgeons are doctors who go inside the body to fix organs and tissues physically. Surgery often involves moving, cutting, or attaching parts inside the body.

BEST JOB IN WORLD!

Most doctors work with living people, but pathologists (puh-THALL-uh-jists) specialize in examining people who have died, in order to figure out what caused their deaths.

MICROBES

You may not know it, but you're not the only one living in your own body. Your body is home to trillions of microscopic organisms that live on and inside it. These guests are not parasites. They don't harm you, and in fact many of them are helpful. Most of these guests are bacteria, but there are also fungi and even harmless, many-legged mites. The microbes living on and in your body are called normal flora.

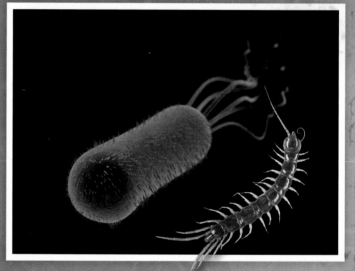

Escherichia coli (E. coli) is one type of the bacteria that live in human intestines. This bacterium breaks down lactose, a sugar found in milk. Some strains of E. coli can cause illness if they get inside your body.

In your guts

Many microscopic organisms live in your digestive system, especially in the large intestine. The bacteria in the large intestine help you digest food by breaking down carbohydrates and proteins that your body's own enzymes can't digest. They also make vitamins B and K out of raw materials in the food.

On your skin

Your skin has bacteria and other microbes living all over it. That's not a bad thing. The normal bacteria found there aren't harmful to healthy people. They can even be beneficial by keeping disease-causing microbes from taking up residence. However, they can cause infections in people with weak immune systems. They sometimes also cause problems if they get into the bloodstream through a cut or other wound.

NOT NECESSARILY ZOMBIE-RELATED

There are actually more harmless microbes living on and in your body than there are cells in your body. But because bacteria are much smaller than human cells, they don't take up much space.

Staphylococcus epidermidis is one type of the bacteria that live on the surface of the skin.

MIGHT WANT TO WASH HUMAN BEFORE EATING

CORD BREAKERS

just a few of the records set by human bodies.

st

...man ever was Robert Wadlow, who lived
...1940. He was almost nine feet tall (8 feet 11.1
...exact). A problem with his pituitary gland, part
...ine system, caused his body to make too much
...e called human growth hormone, or HGH.

...es are smaller on average than men's, but the
...n in history was not far behind Robert Wadlow
...name was Trijntje Keever, and she lived nearly
...in the Netherlands. Trijntje Keever grew to be
...s tall.

FEED WHOLE FAMILY!

Robert Wadlow

Smallest

The smallest full-grown human ever measured is
Khagendra Thapa Magar, a man born in 1992 in the
Himalayan country of Nepal. His full-grown height is
1 foot 10 inches, and he weighs only 10 pounds.

Oldest

The longest-living human so far was a French woman named Jeanne Calment. She was born in 1875. At that time neither the telephone nor the electric light had been invented, and Ulysses S. Grant was president of the United States. Jeanne Calment died in France in 1997 at the age of 122 years, 164 days.

Jeanne Calment

Usain Bolt

FASTEST KNOWN ZOMBIE (LOOK AT HIM GO!)

Fastest

LEAVE SPRINTERS ALONE NOT WORTH TROUBLE

The current holder of the title of world's fastest person goes to Usain Bolt of Jamaica. In 2009 he set the world speed record by running 100 meters (109 yards) in 9.58 seconds. That's a sprinting speed of just over 23 mph.

ISBN 978-0-545-24979-9
10 9 8 7 6 5 4 3 2 1   10 11 12 13 14
Printed in the USA   40
First printing, September 2010
10769

A Zombie's Guide to the Human Body produced by becker&mayer!
11120 NE 33rd Place, Suite 101
Bellevue, WA 98004
www.beckermayer.com

Written by Paul Beck
Edited by Ben Grossblatt
Cover designed by Kay Petronio
Designed by Rosanna Brockley
Design assistance by Cortny Helmick, Tyler Freidenrich, Ryan Hobson, and Sam Trout
Photo research by Zena Chew
Production management by Larry Weiner
Special thanks to Michelle Villarta, MD

Illustration credits: Andreas Meyer/Shutterstock: cover, title page, pages 51, 79, 81, 88, back cover. Max Delson/iStockphoto: pages 2, 30, 35, 38, 45. Mopic/Shutterstock: page 4. jangeltun/iStockphoto: page 6. Eraxion/iStockphoto: pages 6, 38, 42, 49, 63, 72. Ryan Pike/Dreamstime: page 7. Red Frog/iStockphoto: page 8. Nucleus Medical Art, Inc./Getty Images: page 9 (knee). Craig Zuckerman and Jennifer Fairman: pages 9, 17, 20, 26, 31, 39, 40, 46, 47, 48, 49, 54, 55, 66. Mads Abildgaard/iStockphoto: pages 11, 61. SS Serg/Shutterstock: page 12. Sebastian Kaulitzki/Shutterstock: pages 13, 25, 27, 49, 64, 65, 68, 76, 77, 87, back cover. Linda Bucklin/Dreamstime: page 14. Raycat/iStockphoto: page 15. KandasamyM/Dreamstime: pages 16, 36, 71. BSIP/Photo Researchers, Inc.: page 19. Andrea Danti/Shutterstock: pages 22, 33, 52. dreep/Dreamstime: page 23. Tyler Freidenrich: pages 28, 34. EmeCeDesigns/Shutterstock: page 29. blamb/Shutterstock: page 32. Matthias Haas/iStockphoto: page 44. pukrufus/iStockphoto: page 46. Anatomical Design/Shutterstock: pages 50, 59. mmutlu/Shutterstock: page 50. sgame/iStockphoto: page 50. Gnanavel Subramani/Dreamstime: page 53. melhi/iStockphoto: page 53. Mike Saunders/Getty Images: page 56. Oguz Aral/Shutterstock: pages 57, 58. Btarski/Wiki Commons: page 59. Matthew Cole/Shutterstock: page 70. Henrik Jonsson/iStockphoto: page 72. Knorre/Shutterstock: page 72. luchschen/Shutterstock: back cover.

Photo credits: Page 2: Professor Zombie © Ian McDonnell/iStockphoto. Page 4: Zombie man © kkgas/iStockphoto. Page 5: Two zombies © Peter Macdiarmid/Getty Images News. Page 7: Zombie twins © Gareth Cattermole/Getty Images Entertainment. Page 8: Zombie man © Scott Griessel/Dreamstime. Page 9: Toast © Stuart Burford/iStockphoto; humerus bone © DWithers/iStockphoto. Page 11: Zombie man © DeGrie Photo/iStockphoto. Page 12: Zombie woman © S.M./Shutterstock. Page 13: Vertebra © DWithers/iStockphoto; hand © sbayram/iStockphoto. Page 14: Zombie woman © Glovatskiy/Shutterstock. Page 15: Zombie handshake © Ian McDonnell. Page 16: Professor Zombie © Ian McDonnell. Page 17: Artificial hip © 33karen33/iStockphoto. Page 18: Zombie hand © jrroman/iStockphoto; adult and child hand X-rays © SPL/Photo Researchers, Inc. Page 19: Zombie girl © Nathan Marx/istockphoto. Page 21: Zombie man © Dmytro Konstantynov/Dreamstime; closed fracture © belterz/iStockphoto; open fracture © emmy-images/iStockphoto; comminuted fracture © thesleepless1/iStockphoto; greenstick fracture © czardases/iStockphoto; surgical screws © choja/iStockphoto. Page 22: Rotten teeth © hidesy/iStockphoto. Page 24: Spoon in jam © TSchon/iStockphoto. Page 25: Zombie woman © Ian McDonnell. Page 26: Zombie boy © Ccharleson/Dreamstime. Page 27: Zombie man © Ian McDonnell. Page 29: Meat © mdesign.se/iStockphoto. Page 30: Zombie woman © KCline/iStockphoto. Page 31: Meat © Peter Polak/iStockphoto. Page 33: Zombie woman © sumografika/iStockphoto. Page 34: Zombie woman © Ian McDonnell. Page 36: Toasting with blood © James Brey/iStockphoto. Page 37: Used bandage © Feng Yu/Dreamstime. Page 38: Zombie © Malcolm Taylor/Getty Images Entertainment. Page 40: Eyeball pasta © redmonkey8/iStockphoto. Page 41: Zombie boy © jane/iStockphoto. Page 43: Zombie boy © Ccharleson. Page 47: Zombies © Ian McDonnell. Page 50: Zombie man © airportrait/iStockphoto. Page 52: Tin of eyeballs © siloto/iStockphoto. Page 53: Glasses mummy © ferrantraite/iStockphoto. Page 55: Zombies © Renphoto/iStockphoto. Page 56: Zombie woman © Ian McDonnell. Page 58: Zombie man © Simon Podgorsek/iStockphoto. Page 60: Zombie woman © William Attard McCarthy/Shutterstock. Page 62: Zombie man © Sergeytitov/Dreamstime. Page 63: Fingers and pencil photographed by Sarah Baynes. Page 65: Zombie man © kkgas. Page 67: Zombie man © Ian McDonnell; cilia in the lung © Dr. David Phillips/Visuals Unlimited/Getty Images. Page 69: Vocal folds © James P. Thomas, MD; zombie on the phone © Getty Images Entertainment. Page 70: Zombie man © Creatista/Shutterstock. Page 71: Hairy zombie © Dmitry Mordolff/iStockphoto. Page 73: Zombie woman © Scott Griessel; scary cat © wildcat78/iStockphoto. Page 75: Lemon © Anyka/iStockphoto; zombie woman © Ivan Bliznetsov/Dreamstime. Page 76: Zombie man © Dmytro Konstantynov. Page 77: Mouth © Ilya Andriyanov/Shutterstock; zombie man © Kutt Niinepuu/Dreamstime; screaming zombie woman © Greg Wood/AFP/Getty Images. Page 79: MRI photo © lucato/iStockphoto; zombie man © airportrait; ultrasound transducer © zilli/iStockphoto. Page 80: Zombie woman © Ian McDonnell. Page 81: Zombie man © Creatista. Page 82: Zombie dancer © Dmytro Konstantynov. Page 83: Zombie boy © Matthew Rambo/iStockphoto; lunging zombie © LeggNet/iStockphoto. Page 85: Zombie doctor © kkgas. Page 86: E. coli © Luis Molina/iStockphoto. Page 87: Smiling zombie © Brendon Thorne/Getty Images Entertainment. Page 88: Robert Wadlow © Imagno/Hulton Archive/Getty Images; KT Magar © Paula Bronstein/Getty Images News. Page 89: Jeanne Calment © George Gobet/AFP/Getty Images; Usain Bolt © Brunel University/flickr. Page 90: Clavicle bone © DWithers. Page 96: Professor Zombie © Ian McDonnell; favorite niece © Ateo Fiel/flickr; brain origami photographed by Sarah Baynes.

GLOSSARY

alveolus (al-vee-OH-lus): A tiny sac in the lungs; oxygen enters the bloodstream from the lungs and carbon dioxide leaves the bloodstream and enters the lungs through the alveoli.

brain stem: One of the three main parts of the brain, responsible for involuntary movements.

cartilage (KART-uh-lidge): A rubbery tissue found between vertebrae, inside joints, and in the nose and outer ear.

cell: The basic building block of all living things.

cerebellum (sare-uh-BELL-um): One of the three main parts of the brain, responsible for coordinating voluntary movement.

cerebrum (suh-REE-brum): One of the three main parts of the brain, responsible for controlling voluntary movement and sensing.

chromosome (KRO-muh-some): Strand of DNA.

chyme (KIME): Partly digested food that leaves the stomach and enters the small intestine.

coccyx (KOK-siks): The lower part of the spine, also called the tailbone.

corpus callosum (KOR-pus kuh-LO-sum): A band of fibers that connects the two hemispheres of the brain.

cortex: The outer layer of certain organs or body parts, like the cerebrum and the kidney.

diaphragm (DIE-uh-fram): A breathing muscle that contracts and relaxes in the chest cavity.

DNA, deoxyribonucleic (dee-OX-ee-RY-bo-new-CLAY-ik) acid: A long molecule with the shape of a twisted ladder inside chromosomes; it contains genes.

gene (JEEN): A sequence of DNA that makes a specific trait in an organism.

gland: An organ that releases something, such as a hormone, into the body.

growth plate: The part of a long bone where the bone grows longer.

gyrus (JYE-rus): A rounded bump on the wrinkled surface of the cerebral cortex.

hydrochloric (HI-dro-CLOR-ik) acid: A powerful acid in the stomach that breaks down food so that it can be digested.

iris: The colored ring in the eye that controls how much light enters the eye.

larynx (LAIR-inks): The body part that contains the vocal folds (vocal cords); also called the voice box.

ligament: Tough tissue that connects bones.

lymph (LIMF): A liquid containing white blood cells sent to the bloodstream by the lymphatic system.

peristalsis (PEAR-uh-STALL-sis): The waves of muscle contractions that send food through the intestines.

proprioception (PRO-pree-oh-sep-shin): The sense responsible for letting you know the positions of parts of your body.

pupil: The opening in the iris that lets light into the eye.

retina (RET-nuh): The inner surface of the back of the eyeball; light hits the retina and the retina sends signals along the optic nerve.

sulcus (SUL-kus): A groove in the wrinkled surface of the cerebral cortex.

synapse (SIN-aps): The tiny gap between two nerve cells.

tendon: Tough tissue that connects muscles to bones.

vertebra (VER-tuh-bruh): A bone of the spine; the spinal cord passes through openings in the vertebrae.

Index

ME 🖤

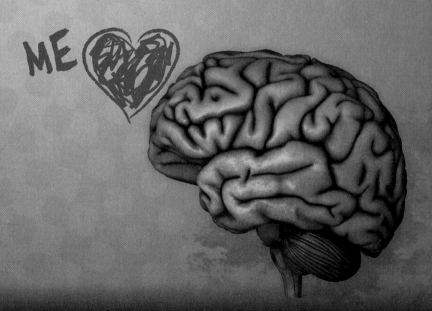

BONUS: GALLBLADDER!

ME HOPE THIS BOOK HELP YOU, MY FELLOW ZOMBIE, TO BETTER UNDERSTAND HUMANS—THEIR BEHAVIOR AS WELL AS THEIR DELICIOUS BRAINS.

I BEEN INTERESTED IN HUMANS AND BRAINS FOR MANY YEARS. ME HAPPY TO SHARE MY KNOWLEDGE SO YOU CAN BE BEST ZOMBIE YOU CAN BE.

PROFESSOR ZOMBIE
(ME FORGET REAL NAME)

MY COLLECTION OF BRAIN ORIGAMI. MOST PRIZED POSSESSION.

ME DEDICATE BOOK TO FAVORITE NIECE. HER NAME UNGGH.